Bann

MW01282092

Learn How To Strengthen Aura, Balance Chakras, Radiate Energy And Awaken Your Spiritual Power Through Chakra Meditation

Daniel Smith

Table of Contents

Introduction

What are chakras? Our body has several energy centers known as chakras. These energy centers are connected to our aura. The aura is an atmosphere that surrounds a person, thing or place that is not visible to the human eyes usually. The chakras allow energy to move in and out of our aura. The chakras and aura affect the subtle body which include the physical, mental, emotional and spiritual body.

The word chakra literally translates to mean "spinning wheel" or"disk". Chakras may look like a funnel or lotus flower when you visualize them. You may view them slightly different in your visualization or intuition of them.

When the energy of a chakra is blocked, such as by being underactive or overactive, you may experience imbalance and illness in that area because the energy is not flowing properly. When all chakras are aligned and active, you will feel healthy, happy and in a state of flow with universal energy. You will have energy and feel an excitement and joy about life.

You may have one chakra blocked or several chakras misaligned. When one chakra is underactive, it may cause other chakras to be over active instead of balanced. There are a few different ways to see if your chakra is blocked. There are several sites online where you can take a free test to see which chakras are aligned and which are underactive or overactive by answering a series or questions. You can find one test below:

http://www.eclecticenergies.com/chakras/chakradotest.php

You could do a chakra meditation and see which chakras are misaligned or not active through your visualizations. You may get a sense that one chakra is overactive or under active. Your intuition will tell you which chakras need more work. This method takes a little more practice. I explain how to meditate more in the "Chakra Meditations" section.

You can also look at the list of chakras in "The Seven Chakras" chapter and see which chakras relate to specific areas of your life that may be out of balance. Once you find which chakras are active and which need to be balanced, you will know which chakras you should focus on.

Once you find out which chakras are blocked, the other chapters describe different ways to heal and balance your chakras. You can try all of the methods or just do the methods that work for you. There are many ways to open your chakras. This book contains ideas to get you started healing your energetic body and living a full and healthy life.

Chapter 1: History of Chakras

The history of the concept of chakras starts in 1700 BCE - 1100 BCE in the Vedas, ancient Hindu texts. Information in the Vedas may have come from even earlier oral traditions in Aryan culture. Guru Goraknath wrote about how to open the chakras through meditation in the Gorakshashatakam. The Yoga Upanishads in 600BC mention the chakras. The Yoga Sutras of Patanjali in 200BC also mention the concept of using chakras as energetic fields.

There is no set or standard system of chakras. There are different cultures that have their own system and beliefs of chakras. Most of these beliefs have the common ideas of chakras being energy centers in the body with their own color and other associations.

In Tibetan Buddhism, chakras are used in the completion stage of Buddahood. In the completion stage, subtle winds of the body are use to achieve bliss. Chakras are especially important in the Indian Vajrayana branch.

Hesychasm is a form of Christian meditation. Various areas, such as in the heart area, are concentrated on during prayer. The different points of prayer on the body resemble those found in the chakra system.

Qigong describes a theory of Qi energy that goes through different energy channels, similar to that of the chakra system. In this system, energy comes up the spine and down through the front torso. It enters various fields called dantians that are located in the navel, heart and between the eyebrow. Dantians are comparable to chakras

In the Himalayan Bönpo tradition, chakras are seen as important and there are six major chakras used. Each of the major chakras is connected to the six realms of existence. Chakras are opened up through yoga and seed syllables.

The theory of chakras was introduced to the Western world in the 1920s. Indian texts called the Sat-Cakra-Nirupana and the Padaka-Pancaka, by Sir John Woodroffe, alias Arthur Avalon were translated. C.W. Leadbeater wrote a book called The Chakras that was influenced by other texts and theories. The Western theory of chakra includes seven major chakras. Modern physiology and technology in science allow us to see these seven chakras physically.

Chapter 2: The Seven Main Chakras

There are seven main chakras. These chakras are responsible for different areas of our life. They are also connected to different colors and areas of the body. The chakras start at the root of your body, near the tailbone area and base of the spine, and end at the very top of your head. The colors of the chakras form the colors of the rainbow when starting at the root. The colors represent different vibrational frequencies that connect to our body.

Here are the seven chakras in order, what area of life they govern, their color association, where they are located on the body, their element association, their sense association and how you can tell if that specific chakra is out of balance.

1. Root Chakra - The root chakra relates to our foundation, the material and physical world and being grounded to the Earth. It relates to money, business, manifestation, abundance and

financial issues. It also involves your living space, physical home, food and survival issues.

Color Association: Red

Location: Base of spine

Element: Earth

Sense: Smell

Illnesses: Fatigue, lower back problems, cold hands and feet, distractions, confusion, cancer

Excessive Energy: Greedy, sadistic, egoistic, domineering

Deficient Energy: Can't achieve goals, financial issues, stability issues, out of touch with body, masochistic

Balanced Energy: Physical energy, abundant, connected to body, feels alive, active and strong

2. Sacral Chakra - The sacral chakra relates to our connection with others, socializing, new experiences, pleasure, creativity, well being, reproduction, power and sexuality. It also relates

to our feelings of guilt, feelings and having the right to feel.

Color Association: Orange

Location: Lower abdomen, below navel

Element: Water

Sense: Taste

Illnesses: Alcohol and drug abuse, anxiety, allergies, sexual problems, yeast infections, impotency, allergies, skin problems, kidney problems, loss of weight

Excessive Energy: Overindulgent, manipulative, see people as sexual objects, emotional outbursts

Deficient Energy: Fearful, abused, self doubt, shy, guilt over sex, overly sensitive

Balanced Energy: Sense of belonging, cares about others, warm personality, clairsentient, intuitive, enjoys being with others, friendly and approachable

3. Solar Plexus Chakra - The solar plexus chakra relates to self esteem, self confidence and a sense of control in our lives. It also relates to humor and intellect.

Color Association: Yellow

Location: Upper abdomen, above the navel

Element: Fire

Sense: Sight

Illnesses: Digestive problems, stomach or appetite problems, feeling overwhelmed, diabetes, constipation, memory loss, parasites, ulcers

Excessive Energy: Workaholic, perfectionist, judgmental, cold and uncaring

Deficient Energy: Lack of confidence, nervous, jealous, can not trust others

Balanced Energy: Self respect, expressive, intellectual, enjoys new experiences, personal power, relaxed, good appetite

4. Heart Chakra - The heart chakra relates to love, happiness and peace. It also relates to acceptance of oneself, self control and forgiveness.

Color Association: Green

Location: Center of chest near the heart

Element: Nature

Sense: Touch

Illnesses: Heart attack, heart problems, breathing problems, breast cancer, high blood pressure, insomnia, cancer

Excessive Energy: Melodramatic, demanding, uses sex to control people, manipulative in relationships

Deficient Energy: Heartbreak, trust issues, loneliness, feeling sorry for oneself, inability to let go of past relationships, indecisive, paranoid, feel unworthy of love, afraid of rejection

Balanced Energy: Empathetic, nurturing, compassionate, optimistic, good sexual energy, peaceful

5. Throat Chakra - The throat chakra relates to how we express ourselves and communication. It is about the right to speak and express oneself. It also relates to honesty and loyalty.

Color Association: Blue

Location: Throat

Element: Air

Sense: Hearing

Illnesses: Throat problems, thyroid problems, neck problems, shoulder problems, hormonal problems, fever, menopause, mood swings, hyperactivity

Excessive Energy: Talking all the time, dogmatic, arrogant

Deficient Energy: Unreliable, uncomfortable with speaking, timid, afraid of sex, untruthful

Balanced Energy: Comfortable with speaking, good public speaker, sexual energy, lives in the moment, centered, loyal, truthful

6. Third Eye Chakra - The third eye relates to decisions, intuition, the big picture, wisdom and imagination. It relates to repressed thoughts and developing psychic problems.

Color Association: Indigo

Location: Forehead between the eyes

Element: Telepathetic energy

Sense: Thought

Illnesses: Sleeping disorders, learning disabilities, coordination problems

Excessive Energy: Manipulative, egomaniac, dogmatic, authoritarian

Deficient Energy: Oversensitive, timid, shy, undisciplined, confused, attached to material things

Balanced Energy: Balanced, fearless, spiritual, good sexual energy, charismatic

7. Crown Chakra - This chakra is about our spirituality, our connection to our higher selves and bliss. It relates to death and wisdom. It is the state of pure consciousness.

Color Association: Violet

Location: Just above the head

Element: Cosmic Energy

Sense: Thought

Illnesses: Headaches, mental illness, hysteria, senility, lack of coordination, rashes, epilepsy, headache, migraine headaches, depression

Excessive Energy: Frustration, destructive, moody, psychotic

Deficient Energy: Depression, lack of joy, sadness, catatonic, stress, worry

Balanced Energy: In touch with spirituality, can access subconscious, intuitive, miracle worker, sense of purpose

By learning about the different chakras and studying them, you can learn how to recognize when a chakra is out of balance and how to balance and heal it.

Chapter 3: Transpersonal Chakras

Beyond the seven main chakras, there are several transpersonal chakras located above the crown chakra and below the root chakra. The theory on these chakras and how many there are varies a little. All of these chakras are related to the higher self above the main chakras. Make sure you are familiar and balanced with the main chakras before working with higher chakras since they are more advanced. Since these chakras deal with higher energy, you have to be more careful when working with them.

1. The Earth Star Chakra - This chakra is located below the feet below the root chakra. It is a good way to start working with transpersonal chakras since it will protect your energy. The Earth Star helps us connect to the Earth and our daily habits. It is all about grounding our energy. The more you work with your spirituality and higher dimensions, the more you should work with the

Earth Star chakra to balance yourself. Our subtle body will be aligned when our Earth Star chakra is grounded and balanced.

2. The Causal Chakra - This chakra is located behind the upper part of the skull. It relates to divine inspiration and messages from our higher selves. It helps keep us calm, serene and present in the moment. It helps us block out unwanted noise and focus. It is also related to out-of-body projection, etheric projection and spiritual perception.

3. Thymus Chakra -The thymus chakra is located between the throat and heart area. It is known as the higher heart chakra. We can communicate with the higher source and universal akashic records through this chakra.

4. The Soul Star - This chakra is located just above the head. It relates to compassion and interconnectedness of all things. It is the link between our higher self and incarnated self. It allows us to connect with other people's souls

and feel love and compassion. It relates to karma and lessons we need to learn in this lifetime.

5. Grand Portal - The Grand Portal is the highest transpersonal chakra. It allows the soul to connect to the higher universe and divine source, infinite energy, other planes of existence, alternate universes or time travel.

Chapter 4: Chakra Meditations

One way to balance your chakras is to do meditation and visualization exercises. Meditation is all about trying to still your mind. To start meditating, find a comfortable place where you will not be disturbed. Turn off your phone, computer or anything else that might distract you. Some people find music helpful for meditating or setting the mood. You could play some gentle soothing or soft music that helps you meditate. You could also play white noise or nature sounds to help you relax. Do other things to make your environment comfortable such as lighting candles or incense or dimming the lights.

You can meditate any time of the day, but some people find a certain time works best for them. Early in the morning is a good time to meditate. Late at night or before you go to bed also works well. Meditating early or late is ideal because you are less likely to be disturbed and your mind is less active. You should try to get in the habit of meditation. The more you do it, the easier it gets.

Sit upright, but make sure your body is comfortable. You may choose to use cushions or pillows to support your body. You can also choose to sit against a wall or on a chair to support your back. Your body should feel comfortable, but not so relaxed that you fall asleep. You do not want to meditate in your bed as this will remind you of sleep.

Set a timer for meditation. You want something that will gently wake you up and not disturb your peace. There are meditation timers made just for this. They use a peaceful sound, such as a bell, to let you know when your meditation session is over. There are also free apps and websites that offer meditation timers. If you have never meditated, try doing 5 or 10 minutes. If you are more experienced, you can try meditating for 20 minutes or even more. The more advanced and deeper the meditation is, or the higher up or more advanced the chakra is, the longer you should meditate.

To start meditating, close your eyes. Take a breath in and a breath out. Continue to breathe in and out slowly. Breathe in through your nose and out through your mouth. You may choose to count your breaths. You want your breathing to be slow and relaxed. As you breathe in and out, try to let the breaths happen naturally. Your breathing should naturally become slower and deeper.

Try to still your mind. The goal of meditation is to still your mind and become aware of your thoughts. If you have a thought, just let it pass. You may have worries or random thoughts about the day or things you need to get done. Do not try to change or control your thoughts. Just be aware of them. Observe them without trying to change them. As you observe your thoughts without trying to change them, they will fade away. Try to just be. Try to simply be present in the moment without changing it. With practice, this will be easier.

To get out of your thinking patterns, one way is to focus on what the body is feeling. When you start to become aware of your feelings, you will be able to feel the subtle energy of your body. This will help you work with the energy in your energy field and become aware of your chakras. When you activate the energy body, you may feel a variety of tingling sensations that may be subtle or very intense. These sensations are normal and just mean you have tapped into your energy body.

To do a chakra meditation, you want to try to visualize your chakras. Visualization means you are forming an image in your head, similar to how you dream or use your imagination. Visualization allows you to focus your mind on a certain image as you meditate. If you are not familiar with what a chakra looks like, it may help to look at a picture or diagram of the chakras lined up. Memorize the chakras and the order they are in.

The next step in a chakra meditation is to energize the chakras. You should do each chakra individually, visualizing each chakra. Start with the root chakra and work upwards until you complete all the chakras. Visualize each chakra spinning clockwise and growing brighter. See a swirl of energy move the chakra.

Since visualizations are different for everyone, you may see chakras slightly different than as described somewhere else. Colors may appear slightly different. The way a chakra looks might be unique to you. When you see a chakra closed you may see a cloudiness or closing of a lotus flower shape. You might see the chakra fold in. You might see the color of a closed chakra as less bright or vivid. Visualizations are unique for everyone. You should visualize the chakras as bright, healthy, spinning and open.

Once you move through all the chakras, you want to visualize all the chakras at once being given energy. Imagine it coming from your breath or up from Earth. See your aura become bright and full of energy. See a good visualization of all your chakras.

You can focus on all the chakras or try focusing on one chakra for a specific meditation. If you know one chakra is underactive, you may choose to focus just on that chakra for a meditation. Here are some specific meditations to try for the different chakras:

1. Root Chakra - The root chakra is all about grounding and feeling connected to the earth and ground.

There are a few ways you can ground yourself. You can choose to stand up as you slightly bend your knees. Put your feet slightly apart and feel the ground. Sink your weight forward a bit and into the ground. Feel your feet connect to the earth.

Another way to ground yourself is to sit cross legged on the ground. Imagine roots coming out of your body, as if coming from a plant or tree. Imagine the roots coming in the ground. Feel the roots giving you energy from the earth into your body.

A hand position for the root chakra can be used as you meditate. Touch your index and thumb finger together. The tips should touch gently. Hold this position as you breathe in and out and start to meditate.

When you meditate, focus on the color red. Focus on your root chakra opening up and your sense of security in the world. Focus on how connected and safe you feel. Meditate for several minutes, concentrating on this feeling.

2. Sacral Chakra - Sit on your knees as you meditate. Make sure your back is straight and lay your hands on your lap with your palms up. Place your right hand over your left so the left hand is underneath and the right hand is on top. The thumbs should touch.

Imagine the color orange and see orange light coming out of your sacral chakra. Focus on pleasure, sensuality and your sexuality. Meditate on your feelings of pleasure.

3. Solar Plexus Chakra - For this meditation, sit on your knees with your back straight. Put your hands near your stomach. Press your hands together and have the fingers touch each other with the thumbs crossed. Straighten your fingers so they are pointed away from you.

See the color yellow coming out of your solar plexus. Imagine it shining brightly. Focus on issues of self esteem and self confidence. Focus on how you can feel a sense of control in your life.

4. Heart Chakra - Sit cross legged with your back straight. Put your right hand in front of your heart and let your left hand rest on your knee. Touch your index and thumb fingers for both left and right hands.

For your heart chakra, imagine the color green. Focus on what the heart chakra stands for and meditate on feelings of love and compassion.

5. Throat Chakra - Sit on your knees to meditate for your throat chakra. Cross your fingers on the inside of your hands. Have your thumbs uncrossed and touching at the top facing upwards. Using mantras or sound is good for your throat chakra since you will be working the vocal and throat muscles.

See the color blue coming out of your throat. Think about how you express yourself, honesty and communication.

6. Third Eye Chakra - Sit cross legged and put your hands near your stomach. Have your middle fingers touching on the top with them straight and pointed downward. The other fingers should be bent. The thumbs should touch each other at the top for this hand position.

See the color indigo coming out of your third eye chakra. Concentrate on your intuition and clairvoyance. Think about your beliefs and let your imagination free as you meditate. You may also try to deal with repressed thoughts when you focus on the third eye chakra.

7. Crown Chakra - When you meditate on the crown chakra, you should meditate at least 10 minutes or longer. It is the most spiritual of the seven chakras so you should spend more time in meditation than the other chakras. Sit cross legged with your back straight for this meditation. Touch your pinky fingers and then cross the remaining fingers with the right thumb over the left thumb.

See the color violet. Focus on your spiritual and your connection to your higher self. Make sure you are grounded in your root chakra when you work with this chakra.

You can do meditations for your transpersonal chakras too. If you are just starting out, you should focus just on the main seven chakras until you are more experienced. Make sure you are grounded and your main chakras are balanced before moving on to deeper issues experienced in higher chakras. Here are some meditations you can try for the transpersonal chakras:

1. The Earth Star Chakra - If you're working with this chakra, do grounding exercises such as those you do when working with the root chakra. Since the Earth Star chakra is lower down, you should work with the feet. It is a good idea to meditate in nature for this chakra. Find a quiet place outside where you won't be disturbed. Touch the ground and earth with your feet and find a place to sit or lie down. Relax your entire body. Visualize bright white light entering your chakra. Imagine the Earth star chakra below your feet and see a cord moving from Earth to your body. Feel the energy of nature as you connect your body to the ground and let this energize you. Sit and breathe for several minutes feeling the energy of nature and how your body sinks into the ground.

2. The Causal Chakra - Since this chakra is located behind the upper part of the skull, you

may put a crystal behind your skull as you lay down to meditate. Imagine white light pouring into your skull and an energetic field around you. Since it relates to divine inspiration and spiritual wisdom, listen to messages from your higher self. Focus on stillness and a calm feeling to hear your inner voice.

This chakra relates to out of body or astral projection so you can also try an astral projection meditation. In an astral projection meditation, the astral body will travel to the astral plane after leaving the physical body.

Do the meditation when you first wake up. Lie down for this meditation. Focus on your breathing so it is slow and steady. Relax your body and start to fall asleep. Get to a hypnotic or hypnagogic state where you are in between sleep and being awake. Keeping your eyes closed, focus on a body part in your mind. Try to move it in your mind without moving it physically. You can move your finger, foot or arm as an example. You want to see a clear image in your mind without actually doing the movement in real life. Once you master this technique, you are starting to take control of your astral body. You want to eventually try to move your whole body in your mind.

Once you are able to move your whole body, make your astral body stand up and walk around the room. This technique takes some practice and you may not be able to get it right away. You should feel a strong vibration sensation as you enter the astral body. Visually see your body sleeping as your non physical astral body moves around. You can explore certain rooms of the house or travel further. You can interact with other astral bodies. You can look at physical objects while in an astral body and see them in great detail. Know their color, specific details and size. When you awaken in your physical body, verify you saw these objects by locating them in real life. This is a good way to know if your astral projection was real and effective.

Return to your body to end your meditation. Since this meditation and type of practice can be dangerous, protect yourself by imagining your body surrounded by white light before you do this type of exercise. Also make sure your physical room your body is in is cleansed, purified and protected so your physical body is safe.

3. The Thymus Chakra - The thymus chakra is closely related to the heart chakra so you can focus on similar issues related to love and compassion. For this meditation, imagine healing energy sent from the heart chakra to the thymus chakra. Imagine an intense blue light coming out of the heart chakra. Feel the calming effect of blue light removing blockages and fears. Imagine a soothing light that will heal old wounds. Imagine your masculine and feminine sides being in perfect balance. As the blue light enters the thymus chakra, visualize a rainbow light and energy coming out of your thymus chakra. Meditate on this light.

4. The Soul Star Chakra - For this meditation, begin by lying down on a mat or blanket. Place one hand on the heart chakra and the other hand on the solar plexus as you lie down. You may place a rose quartz crystal around the heart chakra. Visualize a rose color light similar to the color of a rose quartz. Let it flow into this chakra and let it heal you. Focus on karma and hearing your inner voice. Meditate on the feelings of love and compassion and feel a connection to other people's souls.

5. Grand Portal - The Grand Portal allows the soul to connect to the higher universe and infinite energy. Deep meditation can help you unlock the grand portal. You can do a dousing technique with an advanced healer to see if the grand portal is open or ready to open using a chakra from a pendulum.

Place clear quartz crystals near the feet and on the brow. Make sure the tip of the clear quartz is pointed downward by your feet and upwards when it is on the brow. Hold the dousing crystal, such as a small quartz crystal on a string over the crown chakra.

The chakra is open if it spins in a natural circle clockwise. If it moves side to side, the chakra is being blocked in some way. If it moves counterclockwise, this chakra is not ready to open. If the pendulum does not move, the chakra is closed.

Once you are done with any type of chakra meditation, you should rest with your eyes open a couple minutes. You should feel energized and lighter. If you wish, you may choose to journal or write down your experiences in meditation to track your progress and see what techniques work best for you.

Chapter 5: Affirmations

Affirmations can be used while you meditate to balance your chakras. You can use the affirmations like a mantra. A mantra is a word, phrase or sound you repeat as you meditate. I go more in to how to use specific sounds and music while you meditate in a further chapter.

As you say each affirmation, you want to find a slow rhythm that works with your breath as you say the words. You want to say each affirmation in a soft voice. You can say the affirmations out loud or in your head. Try visualizing the chakra wheel spinning as you say the affirmations. You can repeat all the affirmations or just choose to focus on one affirmation for a session. These affirmations will work for the different chakras. You can also feel free to come up with your own affirmations using information you know about each chakra. See some sample affirmations below:

1. Root Chakra - "I am safe, protected and secure. Life supports me."

"I am secure. My body is grounded to the earth."

"My body is connected to the ground. I am safe in this world."

"I am financially secure and abundant. I can support myself."

2. Sacral Chakra - "I am creative and sensual. I accept pleasure in my body."

"I am connected to other people. I relate well to others."

"I have power. I release feelings of guilt that do not serve me."

"I am a creative force. I express myself easily."

3. Solar Plexus Chakra - "I am a creator in my life. I feel purpose."

"I am self confident. I have high self esteem."

"I am intellectual. I enjoy new experiences,"

4. Heart Chakra - "I feel loved. I give and receive love."

"I am at peace. I feel love and joy."

"I feel worthy of love. I am loved by others."

5. Throat Chakra - "I express my thoughts clearly. I speak the truth."

"I speak up for myself. My words have power."

"I am honest. I speak words of power."

6. Third Eye Chakra - "I hear divine wisdom. I see the big picture."

"I trust my inner guidance. I make decisions easily."

7. Crown Chakra - "I am whole. I am one with universal energy."

"I am connected to everyone and everything. I feel bliss."

Besides meditating to chakra affirmations, you can use the affirmations in other ways. You can write positive affirmations on the mirror, repeat them in your head while you are going about your day, say them out loud in front of the mirror or write them on paper. You want to see or say your affirmation several times a day so you are reminded of it and the thoughts become automatic. Use positive affirmations as often as possible or until your chakra is active and balanced.

Positive affirmations work because they help change your thinking patterns and vibrations. Affirmations will replace negative thoughts you may have with more uplifting thoughts. They also help you focus your mind on the chakras and their meaning. Your thoughts have power!

Chapter 6: Chakracises

Different activities, or chakracises, should be used to balance chakras. Some are physical activities while others are general activities to do. Either way, you can find some activity you like to balance chakras that are problem areas.

1. Root Chakra - Do any sort of grounding exercise. Try marching or stomping. Do squats while you exercise to feel the energy of the ground. Try doing chair pose in yoga or sitting against a wall to work your leg muscles. Getting a good night's sleep is also good for your root chakra. Wear red clothing or surround yourself with red items. Work with dirt or items from the ground. Make art out of clay such as pottery. Try gardening and working with dirt and the natural environment with the ground. If you are worried about money, set up a financial plan and start saving money.

2. Sacral Chakra - Working your pelvis is a good way to work your sacral chakra. Try doing dances, workouts or movements that allow you to move or thrust your pelvis. Try doing aerobics or water aerobics for a good workout that works this chakra. Massages are also great for this chakra. You can either give yourself a massage, have someone else do it or get a professional massage. Do things that focus on pleasure and are sensual to your body.

3. Solar Plexus Chakra - Dancing is a great way to activate the solar plexus chakra. Turn on the music and start dancing. Try working this area by belly dancing or hula hooping to work the stomach area. Since this chakra is also about intellect, try working the mind by trying something new, reading a book, taking a class or doing a puzzle.

4. Heart Chakra - Swimming is a good exercise for the heart chakra, especially breaststroke. Push ups will work your chest area. You can do push ups on the ground or against a chair or

wall. Try doing cobra pose in yoga. Try doing exercises with someone else or spending time with loved ones. Give a hug to feel the energy of the heart chakra. Since the heart chakra is connected to nature, try to spend time outside or take a walk or hike in nature. Enjoy natural scenery.

5. Throat Chakra - Use your voice and express yourself! Try singing a song or singing in the shower. Sing in a group or with other people. Read poetry or try spoken word. Read a short story out loud. Do something that allows you to use your throat and voice. In yoga, do poses that stretch or relax your neck muscles. Try giving yourself a neck massage. Drink tea or gargle with salt water.

6. Third Eye Chakra - Any type of visualization, meditation or lucid dreaming will work your third eye chakra. Try to visualize or use your imagination. Look at the stars and go star gazing. If you want to do something physical, try painting or drawing visions you have in your

dreams or imagination. You can use watercolor paint, acrylic paint, pencils, pastels, markers or anything you wish.

7. Crown Chakra and Transpersonal Chakras - Connect to your higher self to open your crown chakra. Try writing, praying or meditating. Do activities that are spiritual in nature and let you connect to the divine side of you. Record your dreams and visions.

Chapter 7: Crystals

Crystals are natural rocks from the earth. Crystals work by reacting to the electricity in our energetic body. We have geometric patterns inside our bodies. Each gemstone has a unique pattern that can affect the energy in our body in a positive way that can put our body back in harmony. The crystals affect our subtle body. They move and direct our rhythm to align our bodies and restore its natural rhythm. Take a crystal and hold it up to the sunlight. You will see a rainbow. Crystals can be used to balance our chakras because our bodies create this same rainbow energy when aligned. Crystals work their magic by balancing the energetic field in our body.

Crystals have a long history. They were used in ancient Egypt, Africa and Russia as well as in many Native American cultures. Many cultures have used the healing powers of crystals.

Here are some stones that relate to the seven chakras:

1. Root Chakra - red garnet, smoky quartz, black obsidian, black tourmaline

2. Sacral Chakra - orange carnelian, orange calcite, tiger's eye

3. Solar Plexus Chakra - yellow topaz, golden calcite, yellow citrine

4. Heart Chakra - tourmaline, rose quartz, jade

5. Throat Chakra - sodalite, light blue aquamarine

6. Third Eye Chakra - blue fluorite, clear quartz, lapis

7. Crown Chakra - amethyst, Oregon opal, clear quartz

These stones relate to the transpersonal chakras:

1. Earth Star Chakra - hematite, black tourmaline, smoky quartz

2. Casual Chakra - kyanite

3. Thymus Chakra - kyanite, dioptas, pink tugtupite

4. Soul Star Crystals - herkimer diamond, selenite, moldavite, golden labradorite, scolecite, ajoite, metamorphosis quartz, tanzanite, tanzan aura, zircon

5. Grand Portal Chakra - clear quartz, selenite, diamond

You can get either raw or tumbled stones. Raw crystals are crystals that come naturally from Earth and are untouched. Tumbled stones are crystals that have been polished. They are smooth to the touch and often smaller than raw crystals.

Both tumbled and raw crystals are good choices and each have their benefits. Some feel that raw crystals have stronger energy since they are less processed. Some are quite beautiful to look at and you see the cuts and shine of the natural rock. Tumbled stones have some benefits too though since they are usually cheaper and easier to find. Choose the type of crystal that works best for you. You may also decide to work with a mixture of both raw and tumbled stones. For example, the energy of a raw and natural crystal might work well in a certain room in your house while a tumbled stone works well for you in your bath.

Before you use a crystal, you should clear it to get rid of older vibrations and bad energy that might have gotten on it. This method is not that hard to do and there are several ways to do it:

1. Sea salt is an effective way to clear crystals. Fill a bowl with sea or kosher salt and let your crystals sit in them overnight. Wash them in the morning.

2. Salt water is another method that uses the cleansing power of salt. Fill a bowl with water that is filtered and add a couple tablespoons of salt. Leave crystals in them overnight. Let them dry in the sun in the morning.

3. You can use the same method above, but instead of salt, add a couple drops of essential oil or lemon.

4. Smudge the crystals with a sage smudge stick to cleanse their energy. Just light the smudge stick and let its smoke clear your crystals for several minutes.

5. Visualization is another way to clear your crystals. Close your eyes and meditate with the crystals you want to cleanse. Imagine them filling with white light.

Once you clear a crystal to remove bad vibrations, you may also want to charge it. This will enhance its energy before you use it. It is simple to do. Here are some methods for charging your crystals:

1. Use the moonlight to draw energy into the crystals. Leave them out in the moonlight, or by a window, overnight. You can charge a crystal with the energy based on different phases of the moon.

2. Strike a chime instrument several times near a crystal. Let the vibrations of the music and sound clear the crystal. You can say mantras or chant.

3. Place any crystals you want to charge near a clear quartz. The clear quartz will help clear other crystals' energy.

Now your crystals are ready to use.

There are many ways to use crystals to heal your chakras and keep them active. You can meditate with the crystals. If you want to focus on a specific chakra, you can include crystals associated with that chakra. You can lie down in a corpse pose and put the crystals on their corresponding areas of your body so they are lined up with your chakras. Clear quartz is a good general crystal to use as you meditate.

You can add crystals to your bath to feel your energy while you bathe. Add them to your bath water to infuse the water with good energy. You can also put them on the side of a bathtub or in your bathroom to feel their energy as you bathe.

Some crystals are better for putting on the side of the bath instead of your bath water. Tumbled stones are generally okay to use in bath water, while natural rocks are better placed at the side of the tub. Clear quartz is a good general crystal to add to your bathtub as it has an overall cleansing effect on your aura and chakras.

There is chakra jewelry you can wear to balance your chakras. For example, you can get necklaces or bracelets with natural crystal stones included in them. Wearing crystal jewelry is a way to take crystals with you as you go out or about your day.

Another way to carry chakras with you is to keep a set of small tumbled crystal stones in a small pouch. You can take these stones with you as you travel and take them out whenever you need to use their energy or work with them.

There are many ways to add crystals to your life. As you work with crystals, you will find which crystals work best for you and what methods work best for your chakras.

Chapter 8: Foods and Recipes

Eating healthy is important to your health. Choosing the right foods can help your chakras stay aligned. Certain foods are connected to different chakras. You could eat more of a certain food to balance a chakra. You should also be careful not to overeat a certain food since it might make your chakra overactive.

1. Root Chakra - To balance your root chakra, eat root vegetables such as potatoes, carrots, beets, onions or garlic. Foods high in protein are also good. Try eating meat, beans or eggs. If you are vegetarian, try soy products or tofu. Add spices that are spicy like paprika, cayenne pepper or horseradish.

Recipe #1: Mashed Potatoes, Carrots and Beets with Horseradish

Instead of just having mashed potatoes, add other root vegetables like carrots and beets. This recipe also uses horseradish so it has a spicy kick.

Ingredients:

4 potatoes

2 beets

2 carrots

4 tablespoons butter

3 tablespoons horseradish

Instructions:

Peel the potatoes, beets and carrots. Quarter the potatoes and beets and chop the carrots.

Add the potatoes and beets to a large pot full of water. Let boil and then cook on medium heat until tender. When they get about halfway tender, add the carrots. Cook all ingredients until fully tender. Drain the water. Mash the vegetables.

Add the butter and horseradish. You may need to add more butter or milk as needed. Season with salt and pepper. Serve warm.

Recipe #2: Carrot Fries

These carrot fries are a healthy choice for a snack. They use fresh carrots and are a unique spin on French fries.

Ingredients:

1 1⁄2 lbs carrots

1 teaspoon sugar

2 tablespoons olive oil

1⁄2 teaspoon salt

1/2 teaspoon cayenne pepper

Instructions:

Heat oven to 425 degrees F.

Peel the carrots. Cut off the ends and tips. Cut in half crosswise and then cut lengthwise to get carrot sticks.

Combine the olive oil, sugar and salt in a medium bowl. Add carrots so they are fully coated in oil mixture.

Spread the carrots across the baking sheet. Make sure the carrots are not touching. Bake for 20 minutes, flipping the carrots halfway through. The carrots should be tender and slightly crispy when ready.

Recipe #3: Black Bean and Tofu Tacos

These tacos include beans and tofu and are great for dinner. Add your favorite toppings.

Ingredients:

10 tortillas

1 (14-ounce) package extra-firm tofu, drained

1 ½ cups salsa

1 1/2 teaspoons chili powder

1/2 teaspoon ground cumin

1/2 teaspoon ground coriander

1 tablespoon extra-virgin olive oil

1 onion, chopped

3 cups shredded lettuce

1 1/2 cups cheddar cheese

1/2 teaspoon paprika

In a medium bowl, mash the tofu. Add the salsa, spices and a bit of salt.

Heat oil in a large skillet over medium heat. Add the onion and cook for a few minutes. Add the tofu mixture and cook 10 minutes. Add the beans and cook 5 minutes long.

In another skillet, warm the tortillas. Add the bean and tofu mixture, lettuce and cheese. Fold over and serve.

2. Sacral Chakra - To balance your sacral, try eating fruits that are sweet such as strawberries, melons, mangos and coconut. Honey or maple syrup are great choices. Try adding sweeter spices like vanilla, sweet paprika, carob and cinnamon.

Recipe #1: Fruit Salad

This fruit salad is sweet and includes fresh fruits and a hint of cinnamon. Use your favorite fruits.

Ingredients:

1/3 cup fresh lime juice

1 1/2 tablespoons honey

1 teaspoon cinnamon

2 cups mango, peeled and cubed

3 cups of strawberries, cut in halves

1 kiwi, peeled and sliced

2 oranges, peeled and cut into chunks

Instructions:

Mix the lime juice, honey and cinnamon in a small bowl.

Add fruit to a salad bowl. Add dressing and stir.

Recipe #2: Coconut Granola Bars

Homemade granola is a great snack and you can customize the granola with various nuts and dried fruits to make them the way you like.

Ingredients:

4 cups rolled oats

1 cup unsweetened coconut flakes

1/2 cup nuts (almonds, cashews, pecans, etc.)

1/2 cup dried fruit (raisins, craisins, etc.)

2/3 cup maple syrup

1/2 cup extra virgin coconut oil

¼ tsp of salt

1/2 tbsp ground cinnamon

1 tbsp carob or cocoa powder

1 tsp vanilla extract

Instructions;

Preheat oven to 340 degrees F.

Mix the rolled oats, coconut, cinnamon, sugar, cacao or cocoa powder, salt, dried fruit and nuts in a large bowl.

Melt the coconut oil in a saucepan over medium heat. Add the maple syrup and vanilla. Add the oat mixture. Remove from heat. Stir to combine.

Spread the mixture evenly on a baking sheet. Press down to form a large square. Bake 20-25 minutes. Let cool completely before cutting into squares.

Recipe #3: Strawberry Coconut Macaroons

These macaroons are a great treat to make that include strawberries and coconut.

Ingredients:

4 cups unsweetened coconut

1/2 cup strawberries, diced

4 egg whites

3/4 cup sugar

1 teaspoon vanilla extract

Instructions.

Preheat oven to 325 degrees F. Line two baking sheets with parchment paper.

Beat the egg whites, sugar and vanilla for a couple minutes or until the sugar dissolves. Add the coconut. Let the mixture chill for at least 30 minutes. Add the strawberries.

Scoop about a tablespoon size of the mixture on to the baking sheet. Make sure they are evenly spread out. Bake 20-25 minutes or until golden brown.

Recipe #4: Ham and Cantaloupe Salad

The paprika in this salad gives it a nice flavor.

Ingredients:

1 1/2 tablespoons fresh lemon juice

1/2 teaspoon sweet paprika

1/2 teaspoon salt

5 tablespoons olive oil

4 cups flesh of cantaloupe, cubed in to one inch pieces

4 large bunches arugula

8 oz sliced serrano ham, cut into strips

Instructions:

To make the dressing, combine first four ingredients in a small bowl. Combine until blended. Set aside.

Toss arugula, ham and cantaloupe cubes in a large bowl. Add additional salt and pepper to taste. Serve fresh.

3. Solar Plexus Chakra - The solar plexus chakra can be balanced with grains that include rice, pasta and bread. As a snack, sunflower seeds are a good choice. Look for ginger, cumin, turmeric, mint and chamomile spices.

Recipe #1: Mint Pasta

This paste has fresh mint and parsley.

Ingredients:

1 16-ounce package pasta shells

1/4 cup olive oil

1 16-ounce package frozen peas

1/2 cup water

1/3 cup Parmesan cheese

1/4 cup chopped fresh mint

1/4 cup chopped fresh parsley

salt

Instructions:

Boil the water and lightly salt it. Add pasta and cook until tender.

Drain pasta. Add the water to the pot and cook peas until tender and bright green.

Add the pasta, olive oil, Parmesan cheese, parsley and mint. Toss to combine and serve warm.

Recipe #2: Cumin and Turmeric Rice

This rice is great as a side dish or to use as a base of a meal.

Ingredients:

2 tablespoons vegetable oil

1 teaspoon dried turmeric

1/2 teaspoon dried cumin

1 teaspoon cumin seeds

1 cup rice

1 3/4 cups water

salt to taste

Instructions:

In a medium pan, add the oil and heat to medium heat. Add cumin seeds and cook so they splutter and become a light brown color.

Add the rice. When the rice browns a little, add the water and salt. Bring to a boil.

Cover the pan and cook on low heat for about 30 minutes or until the rice is soft and tender.

Add the dried cumin and turmeric. Fluff with a fork and stir.

Recipe #3: Gingerbread

Gingerbread is a great bread that includes ginger and cinnamon. It is perfect for the holiday season.

Ingredients:

2 1/2 cups all-purpose flour

1 1/2 teaspoons baking soda

1 teaspoon ground cinnamon

1 teaspoon ground cloves

1 teaspoon ground ginger

1/2 teaspoon salt

1 cup hot water

1 egg

1/2 cup butter

1/2 cup sugar

1 cup molasses

Preheat oven to 350 degrees F. Grease and flour a 9 inch baking pan.

In a large bowl, mix sugar and butter. Beat in egg and molasses.

In another bowl, sift together flour, salt, baking soda, cinnamon, ginger and cloves. Combine wet and dry ingredients.

Pour the mixture in to the pan until evenly spread. Bake 1 hour. Let cool completely before serving.

Recipe #4: Ginger Pasta Sauce

This pasta uses a fresh ginger sauce. It can also be used over rice and vegetables instead of pasta.

Ingredients:

Pasta such as linguini or spaghetti

1/2 cup butter chopped

2 tablespoons fresh ginger, minced

1 garlic clove, minced

1/2 teaspoon cayenne pepper

1/2 cup freshly grated Parmesan cheese

Fresh basil

1. Boil water with a bit of salt. Add your favorite pasta.

2. While the pasta cooks, add butter to skillet and melt it. Add the onions and garlic to the butter and cook about 5 minutes or until they start to soften. Add ginger and cayenne pepper. Cook about 5 minutes longer.

3. Add the pasta and freshly grated Parmesan cheese. Garnish with fresh basil that has been chopped. Serve warm.

4. Heart Chakra - Green foods are great for your heart chakra. Try making a salad with leafy vegetables such as dandelion greens and spinach. Use kale to make kale chips as a tasty snack. Broccoli, cabbage, cauliflower, squash and celery

are other good vegetables to include in your diet. Include green spices like sage, basil and thyme.

Recipe #1: Green Smoothie

This delicious green smoothie is a great way to get your greens in.

Ingredients:

1 cup coconut milk

2 cups kale

2 cups spinach

2 celery stalks

1 banana

Instructions:

Blend all ingredients in a blender.

Recipe #2: Creamy Cauliflower and Squash

This dish is creamy and delicious. It is a perfect way to use cauliflower and squash together.

Ingredients:

1 acorn squash, cubed

1 cauliflower, cut in to pieces

1 cup milk

1/2 cup heavy cream

1 onion, chopped

2 tbsp fresh sage

2 tbsp fresh basil

½ tsp dried thyme

2 tbsp olive oil

Instructions:

Heat the oil in a large saucepan. Cook onions until a golden brown color.

Add squash, cauliflower, milk and heavy cream. Cook 30-35 minutes or until vegetables are tender.

Add spices. Cook an additional 5 minutes and serve.

Recipe #3: Fried Cabbage and Broccoli

This dish is a delicious way to use cabbage and broccoli. Add your other favorite vegetables.

Ingredients:

1 purple onion, chopped

1 clove garlic, minced

1 potato, quartered

2 sticks celery, chopped

1 cabbage, chopped

1 cup broccoli

1 cup water

1 tablespoon olive oil

1 teaspoon dried thyme

Salt

Add oil to a skillet. Add onion and saute for a few minutes. Add cabbage and garlic. Cook a few minutes longer. Add broccoli, potato and water. Add thyme.

Cover and cook for 20 minutes or until the water dissolves and the broccoli and cabbage is cooked. Season with salt. Uncover and cook a few minutes longer.

Recipe #4: Kale Chips

Kale chips make a great snack and are a healthy alternative to store bought chips or processed foods.

Ingredients:

Handful of washed kale

1 tablespoon olive oil

Salt

Nutritional yeast

1. Remove the stems of kale. Break leaves in to large pieces. Make sure kale is washed and thoroughly dry.

2. In a large bowl add olive oil. Add kale leaves and cover to coat.

3. Add salt and nutritional yeast. Add as much as you desire. Nutritional yeast is optional, but will give the kale chips a slightly cheesy flavor.

4. Add kale leaves to a baking sheet and spread out on a single layer.

5. Bake at 300 degrees F for about 10 minutes. Make sure the kale leaves do not get burnt. Serve.

5. Throat Chakra - Liquids are good since they are soothing to the throat. Try drinking tea, water with lemon or juice with fresh fruit. Eat fruits that grow on trees such as apples, pears, plums and peaches. Salt and lemon grass are good spices to add.

Recipe #1: Fresh Apple Juice

It is better to make your own juice than use store bought fruit. This fruit juice uses fresh apples. The agave nectar helps sweeten the juice without adding white sugar.

Ingredients:

5 cups water

3 red apples, chopped with seeds removed

1/4 cup agave nectar

Instructions:

In a medium saucepan, add water and apples. Leave the peels on the apples and include the cores without their seeds. Bring to a boil.

Reduce heat to low. Add agave nectar. Cook 30 minutes.

Remove from heat when the water is a darker color. Cool before serving.

Recipe #2: Lemongrass Tea

This lemongrass tea will soothe your throat. It uses fresh lemongrass stalks and ginger.

Ingredients:

4 stalks lemongrass

1 liter water

2 slices fresh ginger, peeled

Honey

Instructions:

Cut the green part off the lemongrass stalks. Add the lemongrass and ginger to a teapot or cups.

Boil the water in another pot. Pour the water over the teapot once it has boiled. Add honey to sweeten.

Recipe #3: Plum and Peach Jam

This jam uses fresh plums and peaches.

2 pounds ripe peaches, chopped

2 pounds ripe red plums, chopped

1 1/2 cups sugar

1/2 cup water

1 tablespoon lemon juice

Instructions:

Add fruit to a large pot. Add water, sugar, and lemon juice. Bring to a boil. Let the mixture thicken about 20 minutes.

Reduce heat to low. Cook about 30 minutes, stirring frequently. Let cool completely before adding to a heat safe container.

6. Third Eye Chakra - Look for foods that have a dark blue sort of color. Fruits like blueberries, blackberries, raspberries and red grapes are great to include in your diet. For drinks, red wine is a good choice. Lavender or mugwort are good spices to add.

Recipe #1: Lavender Blueberry Pancakes

These blueberry pancakes are an easy way to add fruit to your breakfast. They also use lavender to give them a kick.

Ingredients:

2 cups all purpose flour

1/2 teaspoon salt

1/2 teaspoon baking powder

1/2 teaspoon baking soda

2 tablespoons sugar

2 eggs

1 1/2 cups milk

1 cup blueberries

1 teaspoon lavender buds

Instructions:

In a large bowl, sift together dry ingredients. In a separate bowl, add wet ingredients. Combine wet and dry. Fold in blueberries.

In a nonstick skillet, add 1/4 cup of batter. Cook on both sides until golden brown. Serve warm with maple syrup.

Recipe #2: Blackberry and Raspberry Jam

This homemade jam uses fresh blackberries and raspberries with no pectin. It is delicious spread on toast.

1 cup blackberries

1 cup raspberries

2 cups sugar

2 teaspoons lemon juice

Instructions:

In a small pan, add blackberries and raspberries. Crush them with a fork or spoon until they are mashed.

Add the sugar and lemon juice. Stir and cook on high heat for 5 minutes. Lower the heat to medium and cook 20 minutes.

Store in a Mason jar or heat proof container.

Recipe #3: Mugwort Soup

This soup is a good way to use mugwort.

3 tablespoons olive oil

1 onion, chopped

1cloves garlic, minced

10 (7 oz) mushrooms, sliced

2 potatoes, peeled and cubed

6 cups chicken broth

8 cups mugwort

Salt and pepper

Instructions:

Add oil to a large pot. Cook onions and garlic over medium heat for about 5 minutes. Add mushrooms and cook 5 minutes longer. Add potatoes and broth and bring to a boil.

Reduce heat to low and cook about 30 minutes or until potatoes are tender. Add the mugwort and cook 10-15 minutes longer. Season with salt and pepper.

7. Crown Chakra - The crown chakra, as well as transpersonal chakras, can be balanced by doing a fast or detox. Incense or sage can be smoked at

this time for purification. The goal of detoxes is to get rid of excess toxins in the body. Detox drink recipes can help your body get rid of toxins while increasing your energy. See a doctor if you are not sure if a detox plan is right for you.

Recipe #1: Lemonade Cleanse

This recipe is part of a cleanse known as the Master Cleanse. To do the cleanse, drink 6-8 glasses of the lemonade while avoiding solid foods.

Ingredients:

8 oz purified water

2 tbsp freshly squeezed lemon juice

2 tbsp pure maple syrup

1/10 tsp cayenne pepper

Instructions:

Pour water in a glass. Squeeze lemon juice in to the water. Add maple syrup and a bit of cayenne pepper.

Recipe #2: Fruit Detox Drink

This fruit drink is high in fiber and vitamins and will help your body detox. It also contains essential fatty acids.

Ingredients:

8 oz of orange juice

4 oz water

1/3 cup banana

1/4 cup strawberries

½-inch slice of ginger

1 small garlic clove

1 tablespoon flax oil

1 tablespoon lecithin granules

1 tablespoon of protein powder

Instructions:

Blend all ingredients in a blender.

It is easy to cook with foods to balance your chakras. You just have to be aware of what foods you are adding to your body and how they affect you on an energetic level.

Chapter 9: Your Living Space

Did you know your house is also connected to different chakras? By cleaning out certain rooms and having an overall organized living space, you can balance your chakras. If one chakra is underactive or overactive, you may focus on the room associated with that chakra to help balance that chakra and get better energy. Here are the associations of chakras with different rooms:

1. Root Chakra - Basement

2. Sacral Chakra - Bedroom

3. Solar Plexus Chakra - Bathroom

4. Heart Chakra - Kitchen

5. Throat Chakra - Living Room

6. Third Eye Chakra - Office, Den, Windows

7. Crown Chakra - Attic, Roof

You should clean the rooms yourself to get the full experience of clearing your chakras. You do not want to just get someone else to clean the room because you want to feel connected to the rooms and energy yourself. To start cleaning the room, get rid of stuff you no longer use or want to remove blocked energy. You can choose to donate or sell items you no longer need to help give it to somebody who might need it. If you have broken items, either repair them or get rid of them. Organize your items. Also do physical cleaning like sweeping, mopping and dusting. Clean windows, floors and ceilings.

You can also decorate your rooms in a way that inspires you and makes you feel at home. If you have had the same color on the walls for years and do not like the way it looks, consider repainting a wall to restore its energy. You could choose to paint it in a color that aligns with the chakras. If you do not feel like painting a whole room, you could add accents of that color to the room through furniture, items and accessories. Try adding a green bowl to the kitchen or a blue blanket to the living room.

You may also do a spiritual cleansing of rooms which helps restore the spiritual energy of a room and gets rid of negative energy. If you ever notice the vibration and energy of a room change if you have guests over, you know that energy has power. A sage smudge stick, such as white sage, can be used to clear the energy of a room. A house cleansing is not hard to do. Just follow the steps below:

1. Start by opening the doors and windows of your house. Turn on the fans. This will help let negative energy out.

2. Light a sage smudge stick. Use a match to light the stick and then block out the flame. You will start to see smoke. You may also use sage incense instead. The energy from the sage helps cleanse your house.

3. Go around each room and wave the sage smudge stick around the room. Get the walls, corner of the rooms and around the ceiling. Imagine the sage cleansing the room. You may

wish to say a positive affirmation or prayer as you do this.

4. Put out the sage stick. Close the windows and doors. Feel the good vibrations that come from the sage. Your house should feel clean and pure.

A house cleansing is good to do every new season or any time you feel negative energy you want to get rid of. Do spiritual cleansing regularly to clear the energy of your house.

Crystals can also be used in rooms of the house. They can be used in different rooms associated with the chakras to provide energy and good vibrations. Do what you have to do to make your house comfortable and free of negative energy. When you have a happy living space, your chakras are aligned.

Chapter 10: Bathing and Essential Oils

How you live in your living space has an effect on your chakras too. The bathroom is a good place to balance your chakras through taking caring of yourself through massage, bathing and essential oils.

To start balancing your chakras, use a dry brush to get rid of negative energy in your body. It will stimulate your lymphatic system to remove toxins, get rid of dead skin cells and unclog your pores. You can find a natural bristle brush with a long handle at health food stores. Start at the bottom of your body and use long sweeping motions toward your heart. Dry brush before you bathe or shower. It is a good habit to do every day.

Take a relaxing bath with salts which will clear your aura. As you go about your day, your aura picks up negative energy. Your thoughts, emotions and negative energy from your environment can affect your emotions. A salt bath will help clear your aura. A salt bath has many other benefits of your body. One reason it is effective is because it removes toxins and bacteria from your body. It also relieves aches from sore muscles and joints.

Himalayan crystal salt is the best salt to get because it comes from ancient sea salt deposits and is the purest salt on Earth. If you can not find Himalayan crystal salt, try using an Epsom salt, but avoid using regular table salt if you can since it will not have the same cleansing effect since it is refined. You can also use baking soda to have a similar cleansing effect on your chakras and auras. Add about 1 cup of salt or a mixture of salt and baking soda to your bath. If you can get to the ocean or sea to swim in, the natural sea salt in the water will have a cleansing effect on your body.

Light some candles to set the mood. You can choose colors that align with your chakras. You may play some gentle music if you wish. Imagine bad vibrations drifting away as you bathe. Let your head clear as you bathe in water that is warm, but not so hot you want to get out of the bath right away. Bathe for a good half hour to let your body and energy get the full effects of a salt water bath. You should feel a light and clean feeling when you leave your bath.

A cold shower can also be effective for removing negative energy and aligning your chakras. There are many reason using cold water is good for your body and aura. It helps energy flow better so you are less stressed and more relaxed. Cold water will help wake you up and make you feel more awake thus increasing your energy and reducing fatigue. It releases endorphins, a chemical that helps you feel good. It improves circulation and removes unhealthy toxins and pathogens. It can help spin and open up your chakras.

Try doing a cold shower alternating between cold and warm water. Go under cold water for 30 seconds to a minute or up to a few minutes. Shower with warm water. Then go back to cold water for a few more minutes to finish.

Essential oils can be added to your bath or mixed with a base oil to moisturize your body. Some base oils that are good to use are olive and grapeseed oil. Use the oil on your skin after bathing. You can use it all over or on the area related to the chakra. You can apply it to your hair as a deep moisturizing treatment. You can also use it on your face.

1. Root Chakra - Use patchoul, myrrh, ginger or nutmeg. Concentrating on the feet is great for your root chakra. Try giving yourself a foot massage with essential oil.

2. Sacral Chakra - Use tangerine, orange. ylang ylang or sandalwood essential oil. A sensual bath can help you get in touch with your body and sexuality. You can even add orange peels to your bath.

3. Solar Plexus Chakra - Try lemon, cinnamon or peppermint essential oils. Use as a spray mist before you go out to gain confidence.

4. Heart Chakra - Rose, rosemary or tea tree oil will balance your heart chakra. You can also try taking a soothing and nurturing bath with rose petals. Give or receive a massage from a loved one to help connect with your heart chakra.

5. Throat Chakra - Oils that will help your throat chakra include eucalyptus, geranium, chamomile and lavender. Try adding a few drops to hot tea or warm water to feel the effects on your throat.

6. Third Eye Chakra - Awaken your third eye chakra with vanilla, bergamot and lavender. Add some oil to your forehead before you meditate to increase visualizations.

7. Crown Chakra - Frankincense, rose or jasmine work on your crown chakra. Massage the oil on your temples before you meditate.

Essential oils come from the concentrated oils of plants. You are connected to the energy of that plant by using essential oils because they have life force and vibrations that can help heal your body.

Chapter 11: Using Sounds

Did you know if you raise sound to a higher vibration, it is color? Sound has power and energy. Since each chakra has a vibration, the vibrational waves of sound can be used to balance your chakras.

Sounds can be used in a couple different ways to balance chakras. One way to use sound is to play an instrument. Try to beat a drum while you meditate to balance your chakras. Breathe in and out with the beat and rhythm of the drum. Imagine your chakras opening. You will feel the energy of the music while you meditate and the drumming can help you get a natural rhythm with your body. Drumming is a creative process that will help you open your chakras. It is especially good for connecting with the root chakra as you feel the energy of the earth.

If you play another instrument or sing, you can use that musical energy to create healing vibrations in your body. Playing music is a powerful healing tool that can be used to align your chakras. Did you know that each chakra is connected to a different note and tone?

1. Root Chakra - Tone E, Note C

2. Sacral Chakra - Tone O, Note d

3. Solar Plexus Chakra - Tone E

4. Heart Chakra - Tone A, Note F#

5. Throat Chakra - Tone U, Note G#

6. Third Eye Chakra - Tone OM

7. Crown Chakra - Tone Ee, Note High B

Another way to use sounds is to say vowel sounds out loud to align your chakras. Vowel sounds are considered to be sacred in some Chinese and Hebrew traditions. They are believed to have more important energy than consonants which break up energy.

To do this technique, start to meditate like you normally would when opening your chakras. Sit with your back straight. Say each sound in a gentle voice and try to find a pitch that vibrates and works for your body and chakras. Afterwards, meditate for 10 minutes to feel the effects of the sound vibrations. Each vowel sound corresponds to a different chakra:

1. Root Chakra - UUH

2. Sacral Chakra - OOO

3. Solar Plexus Chakra - OH

4. Heart Chakra - AH

5. Throat Chakra - EYE

6. Third Eye Chakra - AYE

7. Crown Chakra - EEE

There is also the concept of seed sounds, or bija mantras, often used in Hindu tradition. The seed sounds represent the energy of each chakra. Hindu beliefs say that everything is made up of sound in the universe. This belief lets you use sound to change your energy and vibration. As you speak the mantras, you connect to the energy of that chakra. Try saying these mantras as you meditate:

1. Root Chakra - LAM

2. Sacral Chakra - VAM

3. Solar Plexus Chakra - RAM

4. Heart Chakra - YAM

5. Throat Chakra - HAM

6. Third Eye Chakra - OM

7. Crown Chakra - AH

Music and sound can be a powerful tool for balancing your chakras. Choose a technique that works for you.

Chapter 12: Reiki

Reiki is another method for aligning your chakras. It is a form of alternative medicines that was developed by a Japanese Buddhist in the 1920s. Reiki is pronounced "Ray-Key. "Re" means universal and "Ki" means life force energy or chi so the word reiki literally means universal life energy. The concept of reiki believes everything is made of energy and that there is a universal energy. When your Ki is disrupted by thoughts or negative energy, you experience bad energy flow and negative health. A practitioner will see where someone has blocks in their Ki and use reiki to heal these areas. The universal life force energy can be used to draw power in to the chakras and give you positive energy and better health.

Some techniques used are palm healing or hands on healing. This means the practitioner can do the healing with their hands on or their hands off. The Reiki practitioner will use their hands and ancient healing symbols to channel universal life force energy into your body. Your body will be able to take this energy into its chakras to better align your body and state of chakras. The touch is light and you are fully clothed during your session.

There are many forms of Reiki including Tibetan Reiki, Sacred Path Reiki, Tera Mai Reiki, Seichem, Karuna Reiki, Karuna Ki and Saichim 7 Facet. Reiki is a completely safe method to try out and is a natural way to balance your chakras. Reiki can release stress, boost your immune system, reduce blood pressure and relieve pain. Reiki has many benefits for your body and health.

To start a Reiki healing session, look for a reiki professional. A reiki will be able to open your chakras and get you in better health and alignment. Reiki is great when used in combination with other methods, such as meditation or crystals because it reinforces their positive effect.

Conclusion

Opening your chakras and keeping them active can help you live a full and happy life. Your energetic field is important for your health, body, mental state, emotional state and overall energy. There a variety of ways to open blocked chakras including your cleansing your living space, crystals, essential oils and meditation. When you learn about how to work with your chakras, you will be able to open them up and live in a state of alignment.

Other books available by author on Kindle, paperback and audio

Banned Mind Control Techniques Unleashed: Learn The Dark Secrets Of Hypnosis, Manipulation, Deception, Persuasion, Brainwashing And Human Psychology

Banned Methods Of Persuasion: How To Covertly Convince, Influence, Persuade, And Negotiate With Anyone To Get Them To Do What You Want

Banned Charisma Secrets Unleashed: Learn The Secrets Of Personal Magnetism And How To Attract, Inspire, Impress, Influence And Energize Anyone On Command

Banned NLP Secrets: Learn How To Gain Self Mastery, Influence People, Achieve Your Goals And Radically Change Your Life Using Neuro Linguistic Programming

Banned Law of Attraction Secrets: Understanding The Reasons Why The Law of Attraction Hasn't Worked For You In Your Life and How To Change The Results

Banned Body Language Secrets: Ex CIA Agent Reveals How to Read Anyone Like a Book and Master the Art of Non-verbal Communication

CPSIA information can be obtained
at www.ICGtesting.com
Printed in the USA
FFHW02n1245151018
48823684-52984FF